AN IMPOS——
WHIRLWIND OF
EMOTIONS

Sumera Farman

BookLeaf
Publishing

An Impossible Whirlwind Of Emotions ©
2021 Sumera Farman

Presentation by *BookLeaf Publishing*

Web: www.bookleafpub.com

E-mail: info@bookleafpub.com

ISBN : 9789357445009

First edition 2021

DEDICATION

To Usman 'Hotstuff' Swan - For inspiring me once again. This rejected love is helping me produce books

ACKNOWLEDGEMENT

As always, thank you for all the support Mom and Shabaz. Also Scrappy and Noor.
A special thank you to Aksah who helped me with the title when I was stumped by just telling me how my poems made her feel.
I love you guys. Always and Forever xxx

PREFACE

I wrote these poems as a way to deal with my
heartbreak. I am the giver of unrequited love
right now, however, from my teenage years to as
recently as last year, I was the object of someone
else's love. Now the roles have reversed and I'm
finally understanding how the people whose
hearts I have broken must have felt.

Hotstuff

I realised today that I've never called you by
your name
Before we met, you gave me a name that wasn't
your legal name
It was the name your family called you
But you only admitted that after we met
And yet, I never called you by your name
See I found a nickname for you,
It's my version of McDreamy or McSteamy
And it was given to you because I genuinely
thought you were beautiful
Like the most beautiful man I'd ever laid eyes
on.
And so, I called you Hotstuff
You will always be Hotstuff to me
I think you liked it because you always
responded
Yet you didn't understand that I found you
genuinely beautiful

Dream or Daydream?

Sometimes my dreams and daydreams
are so intense
They have a lot of clarity
It's almost like I'm having a vision
Like I'm predicting the future
Of what is to come
It makes me wonder
They make me wonder
Am I seeing the future?
Now, don't get me wrong
I don't think I'm psychic
But these visions are all about you and me
About 'Us'
And I recall them so vividly
That I hope they will come true

Weird...

I have this weird thing
I've never had this before
It's difficult to explain

I want to do things for you.
Not sexual things
Well maybe sexual things.

It's more that I want to do wifey stuff
Partner stuff
Like cooking you dinner

I had a daydream or maybe it was a dream
It happened ages ago
So I can't remember which it was.
Yet in it, I asked what you wanted to eat
When I asked it was before we went to work

I'm even being a Mrs in my dreams
I'm waiting for you to make me your Mrs
So my dreams and daydreams
Become a reality

Infection

I feel infected
I have been ever since we met
It's almost like you've taken me over
Feelings I have for you are in my every fibre

First you captured my mind
You kept me interested
Then you captured my heart
By making me feel

I laughed. Genuine laughter
Then you encouraged me
My God, that made me love

So I'm infected.
This infection is a disease.
And it has your name all over it.

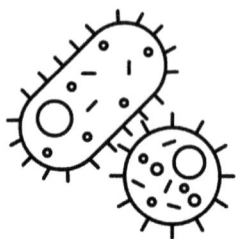

A Woman In Love

A woman in love can't be told she should move
on
She might know you're right
Yet she cannot be told what she should do

She may know it is hopeless
Yet she is hopeful

A woman in love
Is a stubborn fool

Her friends will tell her to move on
She won't, because she doesn't want to move on

She would rather live with the pain of being
unloved
Than give up on the man or woman she loves

The only way a woman will move on
Is IF, she,is ready to move on

Meet-Cute

Meet-cutes are either funny or charming
When we first met, it was kind of comical.
I lied that I didn't have much time
You needed to pee... badly,
Yet we spent around an hour in your car
laughing.
I looked awful drenched in rain
And when we kissed, your glasses fogged up.
I think that's a meet-cute moment.

The second time we met,
Was also a meet-cute I think
I sent you my location
And you almost ran me over.
Completely my fault -
But it was a meet-cute.
Your window came down
And your expression was everything,
You refused to pick me up from there again.

I do think those were meet-cutes.
I don't think I've had them before.
I don't think I'll have them again.

Untitled

I don't need you
I want you
Yet my wanting you is so intense
That it's become as necessary as breathing

Rewind

I often wish I could rewind time
So I could change the course of my life
Not all the parts, but I think I'd try and be a good
girl
Get rid of the bad dating
Do things on my own timeline
And especially forget all the trauma from the
past
It's the trauma's that fucked me up and fucked up
my timeline
And if I could rewind time
Maybe now, I'd be happy
Cause I'd have everything I want
Rather than the missing parts that I pray for

Always On My Mind

I wish I thought of you sporadically
Problem is you're always on my mind
I sleep restlessly, tossing and turning
My eyes open wide
And even in those moments you're on my mind

Is Love Enough?

I often wonder,
It's just one question.
Is love enough?

Many people will say no.
Love isn't enough
It's probably why we so easily throw in the
towel.

I think it depends on the person.
There will always be things you disagree with
No partner is perfect
Perfect doesn't exist

Perfect is a concept
It's the stuff of fairytales

But for me?
Love is enough
And my wasted heart will love you
Until it stops beating

Plot Twist

You were meant to distract me
Nothing more
Nothing less
A distraction from someone who I needed to
forget
But you became my addiction
Slowly...
Over time
What a beautiful plot twist
If only you felt the same

Let Me Let Go

You popped up in my photo memories again
I was already missing you
You popped up with your tiny eyes,
Those huge glasses
That awesome beard
And that cap.

I wish I found you unattractive
For how you've been with me

But you can't choose who you love
Or the reasons for the love

I don't want to love you anymore
I want to move on

It's evident you don't want me
And though my mind knows this
My heart refuses to let me let go.

Worth

Even though I was sad it ended,
I was happy because I finally knew my worth.
Even if you refused to see or acknowledge it.
I knew my worth.
And now, I'll never forget my worth.
Because whilst I have lost you...
I found myself

Love Language

My love language is gift giving.
It's not to make anyone feel bad

I'm just really good at buying gifts.
I remember the little things

I also wrap my gifts
And although you don't like accepting gifts
You do love to unwrap them

It's really cute
How excited you get
When you unwrap a gift
Or know you have to unwrap a gift

I hope, when you use a gift I've got you
You realise how much you mean to me

The Wall

I was dead inside
Somehow... I grew a thick skin
I built a wall around my heart
But that wasn't enough
As I aged, the wall became reinforced
The wall wasn't just bricks anymore
It was concrete
Solid, strong concrete
No emotions could seep in or out
Unless, I faked it.
When you came into my life
Roses bloomed from the concrete surrounding
my protected heart
Then so did other flowers
Before long, my heart was a garden
Living, beating and above all else,
It was finally feeling
Not just love
But happiness, real happiness

Acceptance

I was watching something
Where a dying man gave another guy some
advice
It was about love
Now, those words seemed powerful to me
They seemed true
So I read them
Over and over
Again and again

It helped me decide
I came to a decision I never imagined I would
I would say the words
While saying goodbye
Without fear of pushing you away
Because what's the worst that can happen?

Rejection?

That's already happened!

So I'll be honest.
I'm in love with you
I don't know exactly when I fell in love with you

I suspect it was the time you didn't run me over
You stopped the car before you hit me -
My own fault.
Your window came down
And you gestured get in

I made a promise to myself.
8 or 9 years ago
That I wouldn't tell anyone
If I wasn't certain how they felt
But I have to speak
I have to free myself from the constraints of my
promise

So here goes...
I love you
And I'd do pretty much anything for you,
I'd give up anyone for you.

Not that it matters -
Because you already said no.

Permanent

It was always you
From the first moment I laid eyes on your photos
To the last proper conversation we had
Even with all the 'potentials' I've spoken to
since,
It's you.
You're the one I can't ignore
You're the one I imagine a future with
You're the one invading my dreams
Both subliminally and consciously
I daydream about you and I dream of you
You're in my every thought
You're the only one I've ever wanted to make a
permanent part of my life

Destroyed

I warned you not to play with fire
I promised a small flame could be fanned
Yet you didn't heed my warning
Now you're burning
And all I can do is watch
While you smoulder

Him

But you are not him
No one is him
They could never be him.
And I know you want what he has
What he doesn't even know he has.
But you are not him,
No one is him
They could never be him

The First Cut Is The Deepest

The first cut is the deepest
Carve your name
Letter by letter
On my skin
The biggest choice is where to carve
Should it be my leg or arm?
As long as its deep
I don't need ink
Because the scar that's left
Will bare your name
But what do I use
Razor blade or knife
Intricate shapes need to be created
Don't go too deep
Deep enough to scar
Don't want to pass out
Atleast until its complete
Treat it like a tattoo
Without ink
Ingrained on my skin

Creep

You look so chilled doing your gardening
Snip here, snip there
Tending to those plants
With love and affection
Appreciation all over your face
Surprisingly, you sleep like a baby
Soundly through the night
Barely turning for comfort
I check the clock
Your alarm
It's going to go off
So I take a quick selfie for my collection
You're beautiful you know...
Better leave before you see me
I'm glad we get to spend the night together
Every night together

Milton Keynes UK
Ingram Content Group UK Ltd.
UKHW022035310823
427750UK00014B/402

9 789357 445009